Sexy Coloring Book

Hot Chicks for Coloring

JANE SOLOMON

This page intentionally left blank.

ABOUT THE BOOK

If you've ever wanted to color the most amazing long legged, busty girls of your dreams, the wait is over. Featuring multiple sexy women in seductive poses, this coloring book is a must for anyone who loves to color and loves sexy girls.

CONTENTS

This page intentionally left blank.

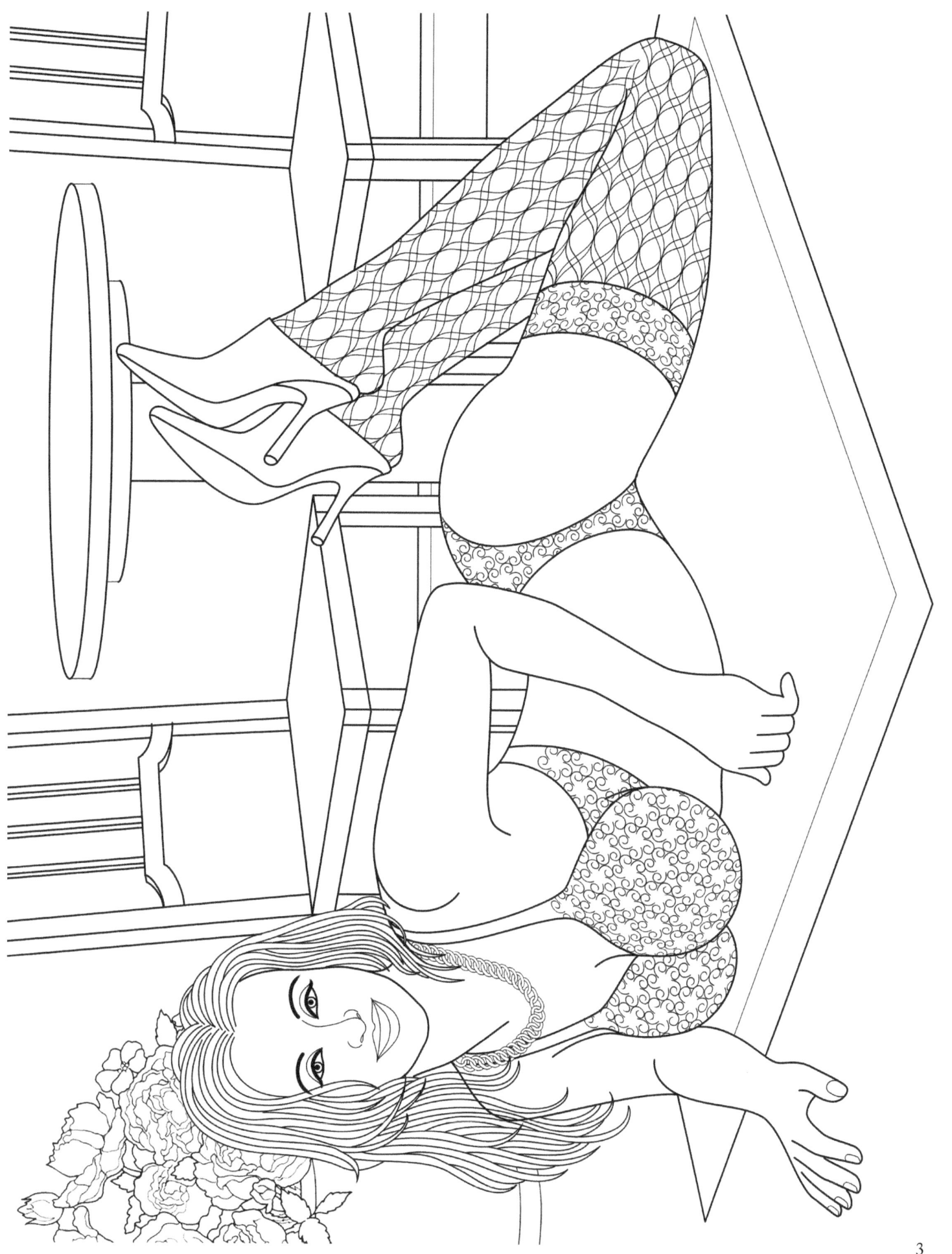

Scene 1

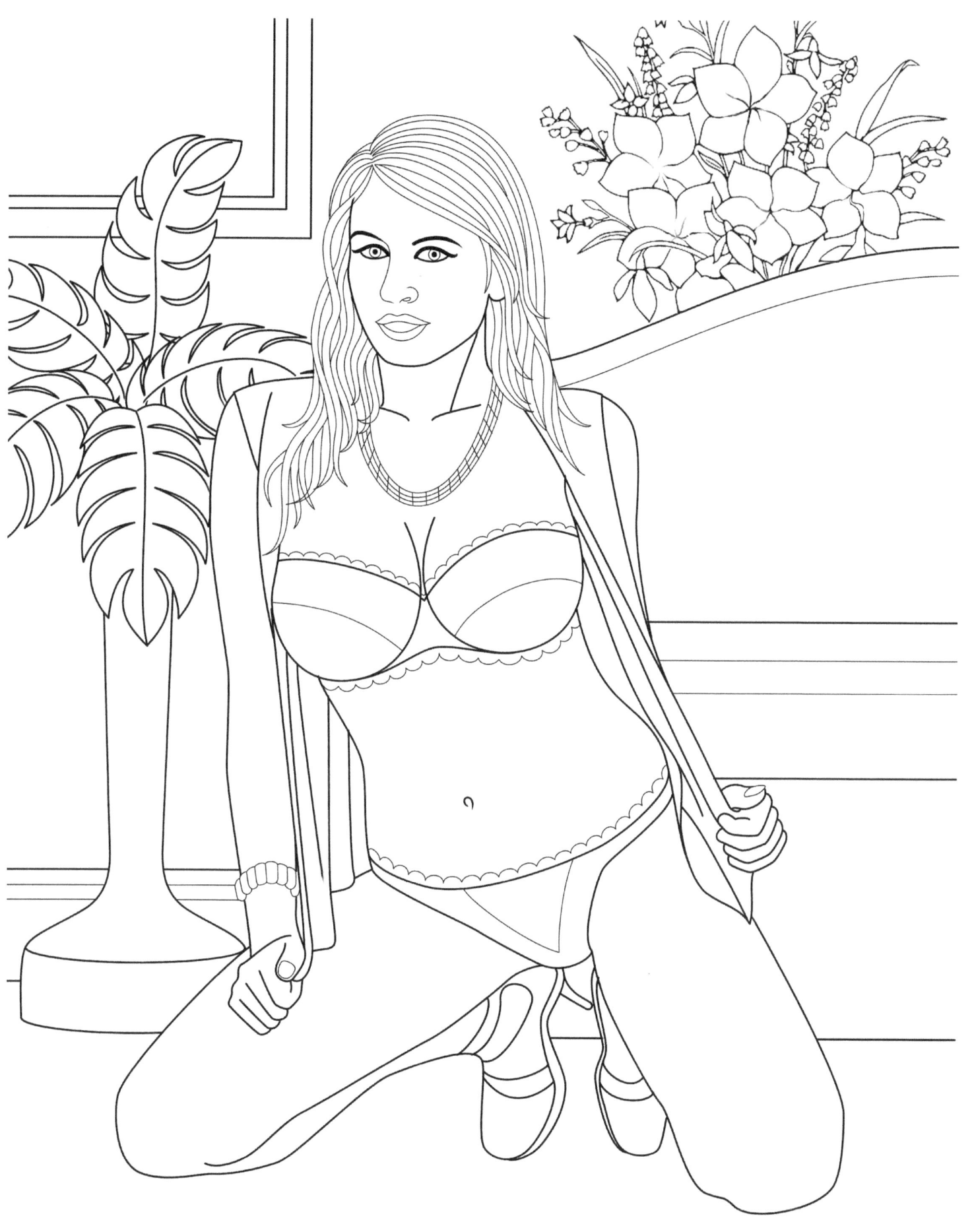

Scene 2

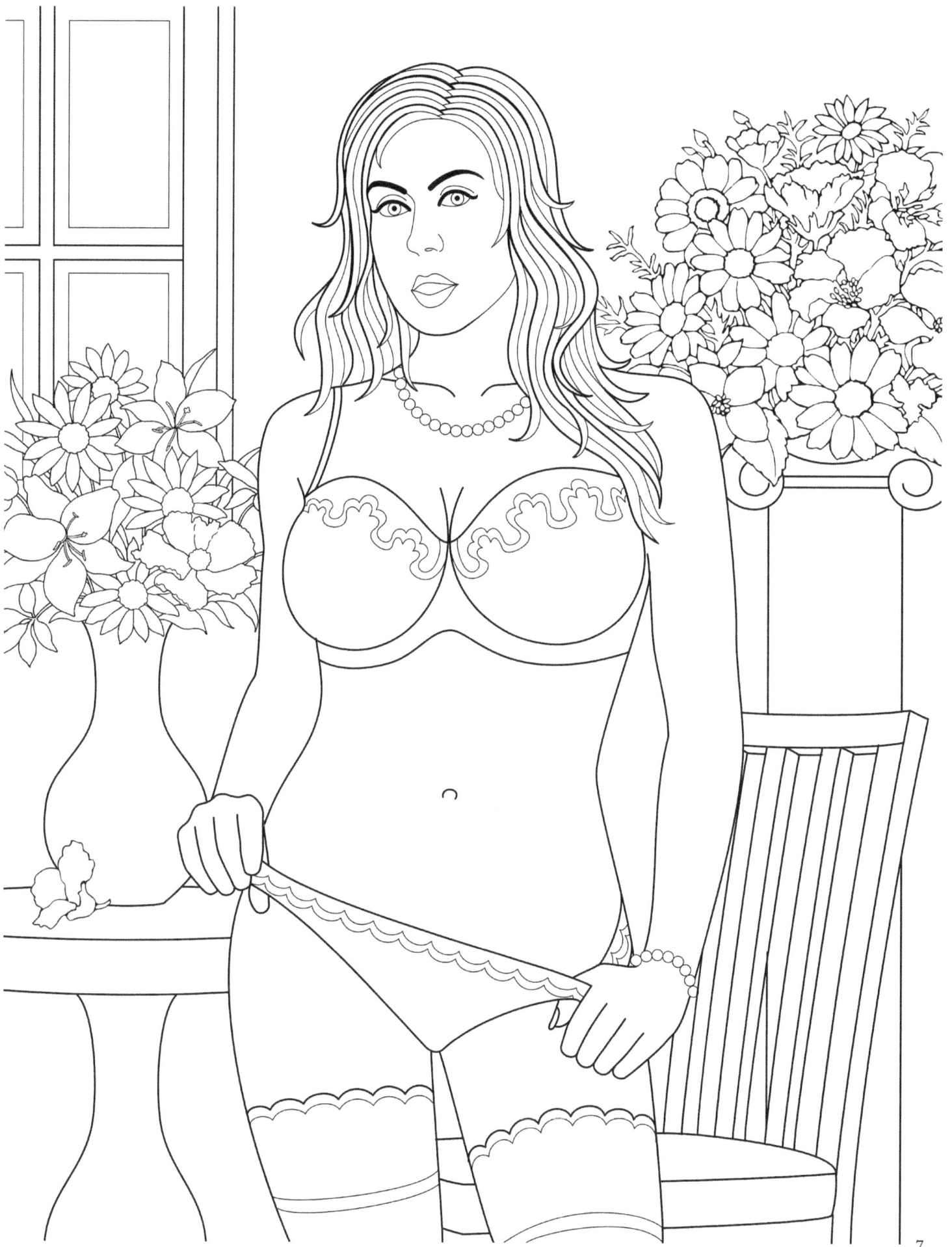

Scene 3

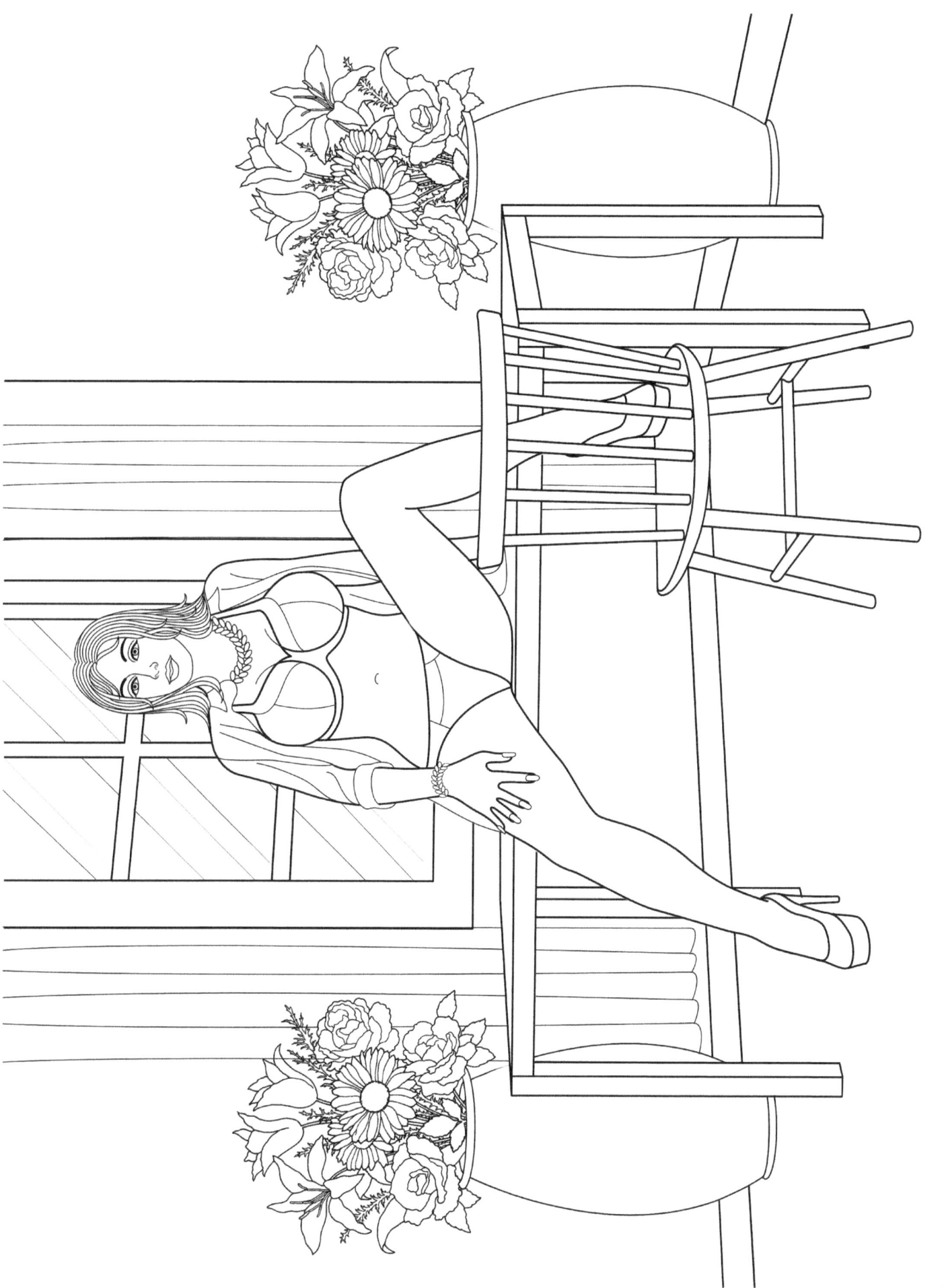

Scene 4

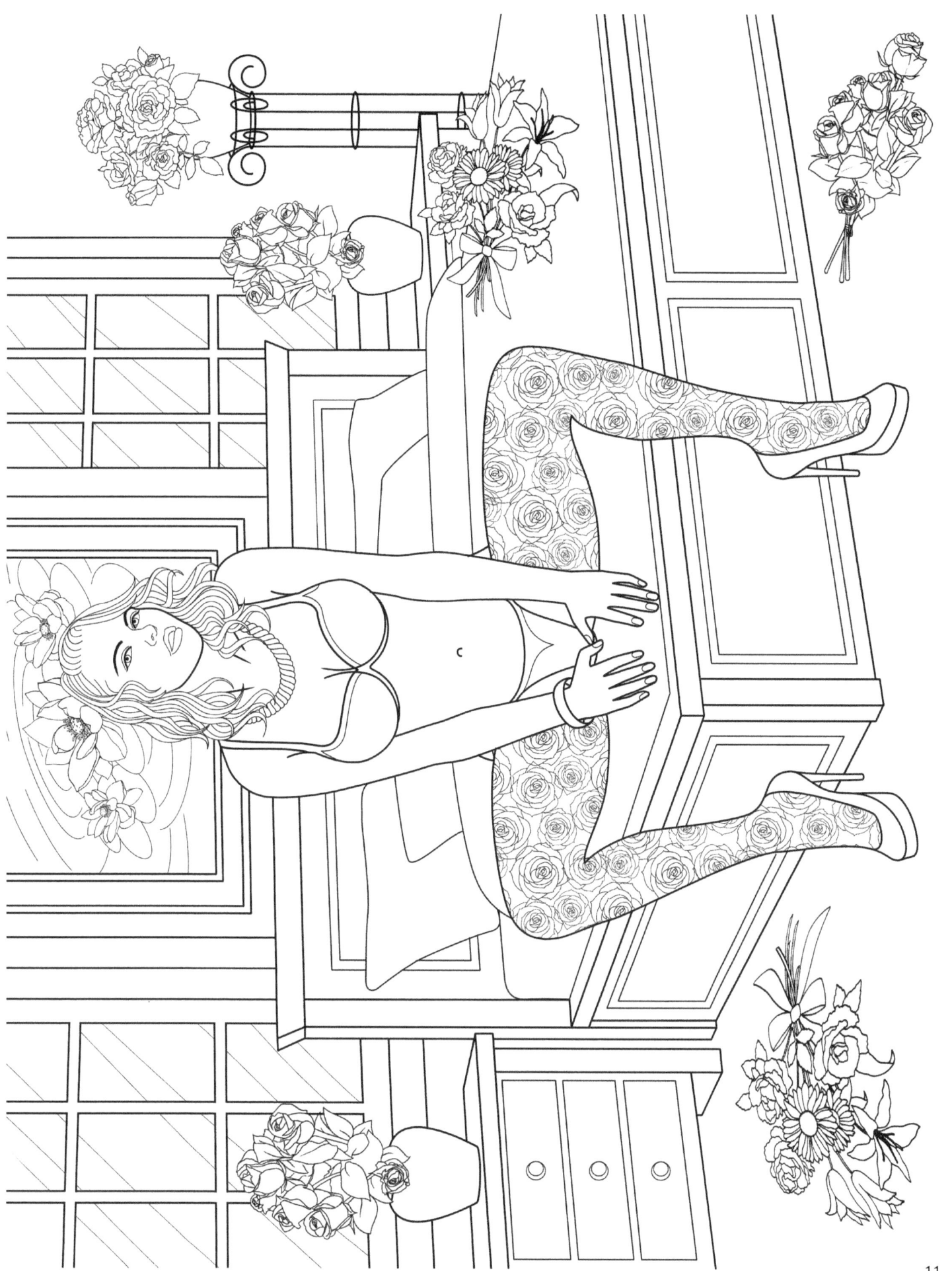

Scene 5

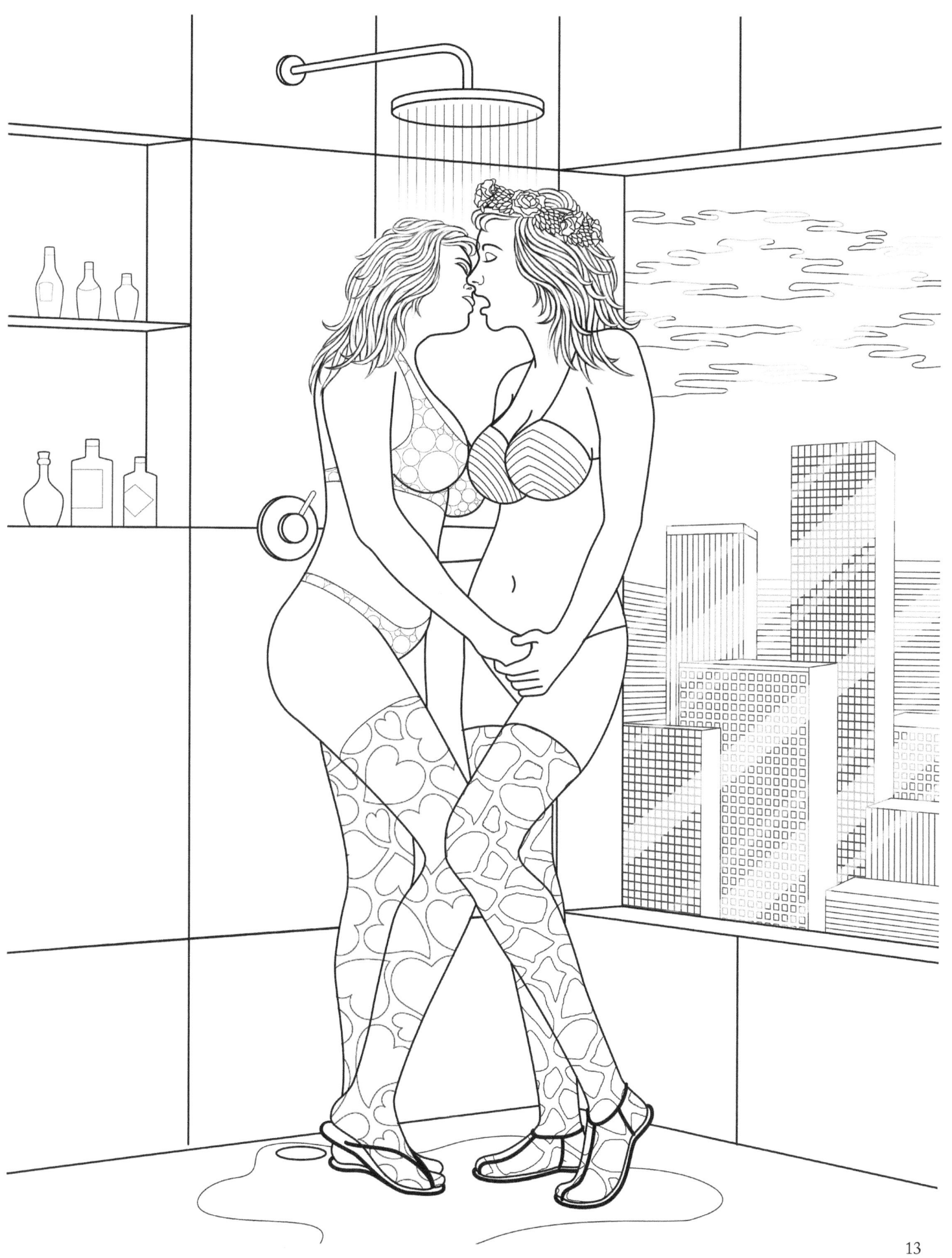

13

Scene 6

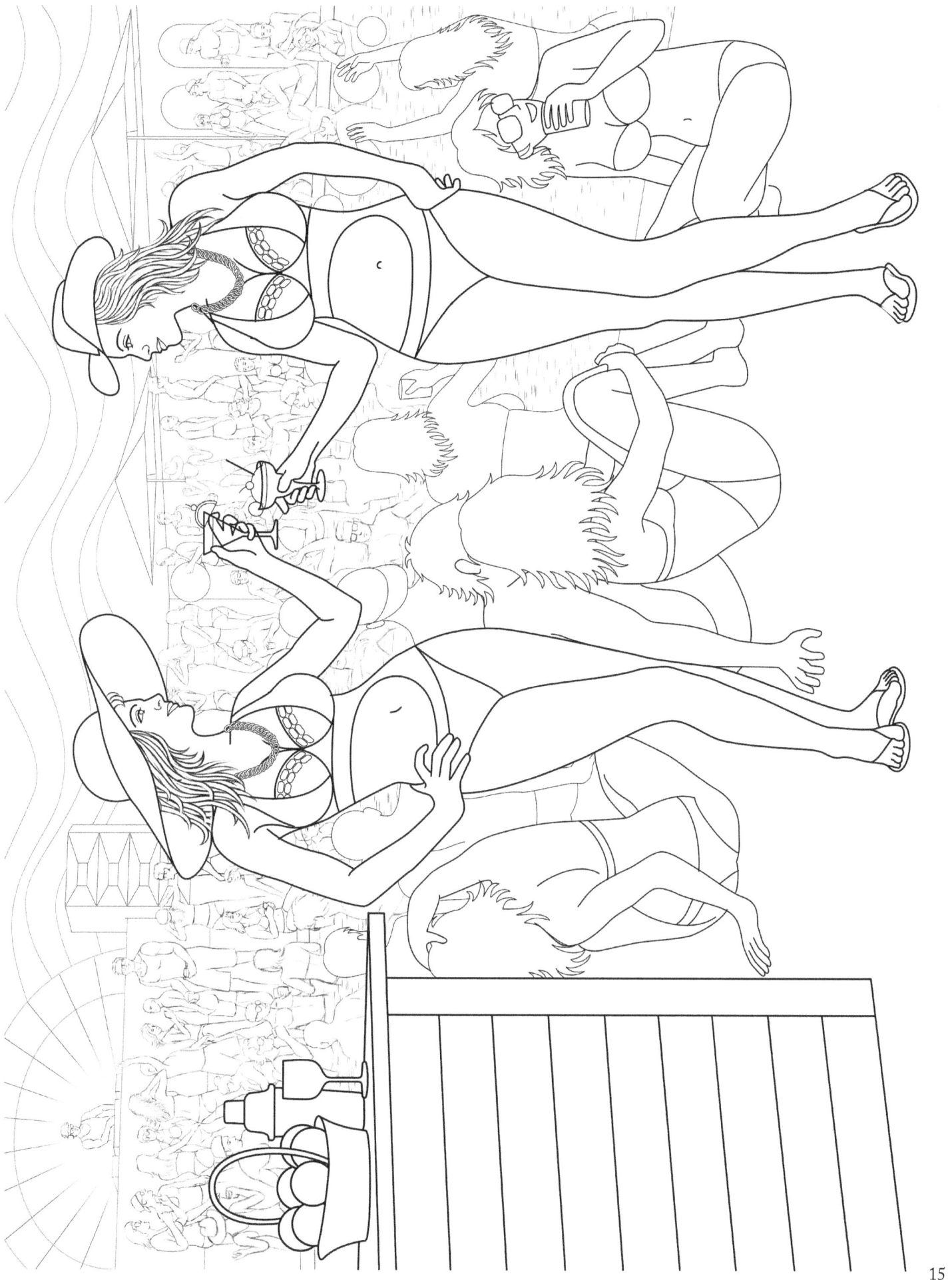

Scene 7

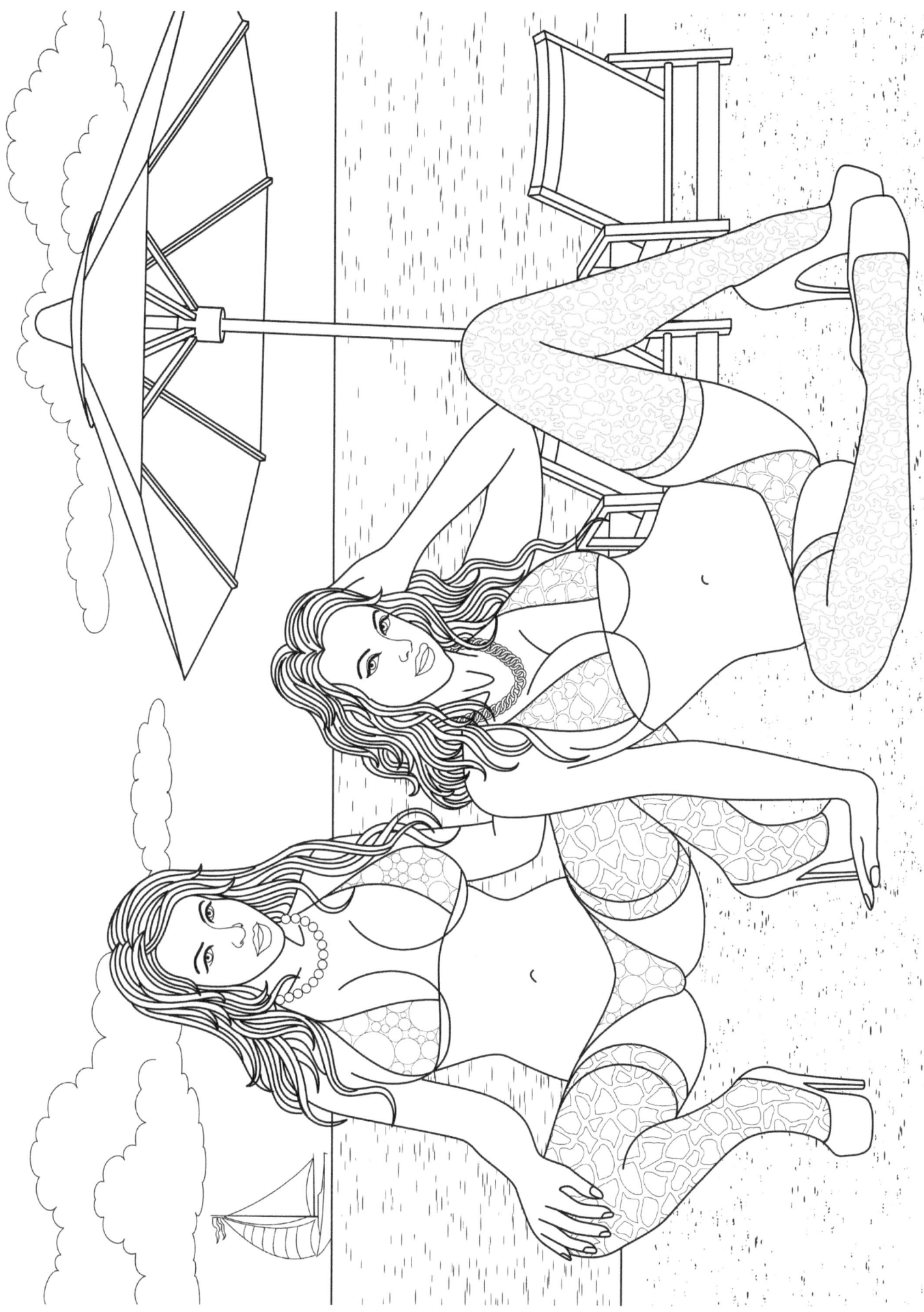

Scene 8

This page intentionally left blank.

ABOUT THE BOOK

If you've ever wanted to color the most amazing long legged, busty girls of your dreams, the wait is over. Featuring multiple sexy women in seductive poses, this coloring book is a must for anyone who loves to color and loves sexy girls.